M000266200

UPSIDE DOWN LIVING

money

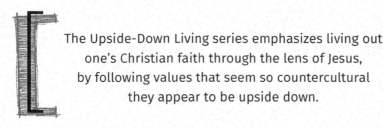

The Upside-Down Living series emphasizes living out
one's Christian faith through the lens of Jesus,
by following values that seem so countercultural
they appear to be upside down.

Leonard M. Dow

Herald Press

Harrisonburg, Virginia

Upside-Down Living
Money

Written by Leonard M. Dow
Design by Merrill Miller
Cover photo by Leslie Banks/iStockphoto/Thinkstock

Unless otherwise noted, Scripture text is quoted, with permission, from the *New Revised Standard Version*, © 1989, Division of Christian Education of the National Council of Churches of Christ in the United States of America.

For orders or information, call 1-800-245-7894 or visit HeraldPress.com.

20 19 18 17   10 9 8 7 6 5 4 3 2 1

MONKEY BUSINESS IMAGES/THINKSTOCK

[Contents]

[Introduction]

"Live simply so that others may simply live."

This popular saying, attributed to Mahatma Gandhi, is quite commendable. It is counterintuitive compared to the predominant values of our Western culture, a culture that consumes and produces 24 hours a day, seven days a week. Numerous resources help readers consider how to live simply, such as *Rich Christians in an Age of Hunger*, by Ronald J. Sider, and the *More-with-Less Cookbook*, compiled by Doris Janzen Longacre.

It is clear from my experiences as a student at Mennonite schools and as the pastor of a Mennonite congregation that the denomination values and affirms living simply. This contributes to the idea and practice of *downward mobility*, the act of moving from one social class to a lower one, that living simply sometimes involves. God gave us an example of downward mobility when he came to earth in the form of Jesus, and then moved from place to place to teach us how to live. Downward mobility addresses quite well what it means to be faithful to God, and it also addresses how we choose to be generous with our resources. It works well when there is the capacity to choose the pace and frequency at which one moves towards poverty, whether for the current generation or for generations to come.

What is often missing from the conversations, resources, sermons, and Bible studies, however, is a perspective from those whose voices are not often heard. Some are struggling economically and, in some cases, have been for generations. So how does our theology and practice speak to building one another up and strengthening those within our congregations? What does it mean to build up and strengthen the larger community?

The gospel (good news) of Jubilee speaks holistically to both downward mobility and upward stability. Jubilee calls those who have resources to engage not just in giving resources as a transaction, but to also act in ways that transform relationships. Jubilee involves naming barriers that often hinder the poor to move toward a place of sustainability, so that there is justice. As this happens, there is movement toward a place of sustainability, bringing both freedom (salvation) and the ability to rest.

Jubilee is the invitation for the church to model God's desire to bring heaven here on earth as Jesus prayed, "Your will be done, on earth as it is in heaven" (Matthew 6:10). Join us as we enter into Jubilee together, allowing it to encompass all areas of who we are spiritually, socially, and economically.

—*Leonard M. Dow*

1:
God's Gift
of Jubilee

Every few months I come across an article in my news feed lamenting our noisy world and the lost disciplines of stillness, solitude, silence, and Sabbath rest. A look at Leviticus shows a key distinction of Yahweh's followers was that they knew how to rest—specifically, a Sabbath rest. The gift of Sabbath rest is in direct contrast to those who worshiped pagan gods and whose earthly rulers demanded 365 days of consumption and production.

Yahweh is just, and provided the gift of rest to all of creation—humankind, livestock, land, and vegetation. Today in the West, we are no longer forced by religion, slavery, or economic forces to work constantly, yet the battle to rest still rages on. It is the voice that whispers, "There is always one more thing I can do; one more thing I can consume; one more thing I can produce; one more phone call, text, email, Facebook post, tweet I can respond to."

> The command God gave to Moses is a needed
> corrective for today: "Remember the Sabbath day
> by keeping it holy" (Exodus 20:8 NIV).

We need to practice a Spirit-led Sabbath rest in which our identity, our life purpose, and our value in God's eyes are not measured by what we do for a profession, what we produce, or what others say about what we do. Rather, our ultimate value comes from trust in the One who created us and compassionately provides to all who seek a Sabbath rest.

"You shall count off seven weeks of years, seven times seven years, so that the period of seven weeks of years gives forty-nine years. Then you shall have the trumpet sounded loud; on the tenth day of the seventh month—on the day of atonement—you shall have the trumpet sounded throughout all your land. And you shall hallow the fiftieth year and you shall proclaim liberty throughout the land to all its inhabitants. It shall be a jubilee for you: you shall return, every one of you, to your property and every one of you to your family" (Leviticus 25:8-10).

God established the Jubilee year as part of the Sabbath cycle.[1] Everyone rests on the Sabbath day, which is every seventh day. Debts are canceled and farmers let the land rest during the Sabbath year, which is every seventh year. Everyone and everything gets a break during the Jubilee year (Sabbath of Sabbaths), every 49th year, including land, livestock, prisoners, slaves, and people in debt.

---

1   See Kim Tan, *The Jubilee Gospel: The Jubilee, Spirit and the Church* (Milton Keynes, UK: Authentic Media, 2008), 6–18 .

DAYS	YEARS	7 YEARS
1	1	1–7
2	2	8–14
3	3	15–21
4	4	22–28
5	5	29–35
6	6	36–42
7: Sabbath	7: Sabbath	43–49
		50: Jubilee

The Jubilee year was a season:

> to trust and be reminded God is our ultimate provider;

> to rest together and worship God; and

> of economic reform, where the land goes back to its original owners, debts are forgiven, and slaves are released.

> Jubilee is not only for the financially poor; Jubilee is also desperately needed for those in positions of power, privilege, and wealth.

Why did God outline Jubilee? First, God wanted the

Israelites to be a nation built on justice. This differed from the nations around them that built their economies on oppressive practices of slavery, servitude, and debt. Second, Jubilee reminded the Israelites that they depended on God for their land, food, and prosperity. The people and the land rested, and God provided. Third, God knew some people would do well with their land. Others, through injustice, mismanagement, or bad decisions, would lose it all. They would sell their land to the rich, and sometimes sell themselves or family members into slavery to pay

their debts. God wanted to prevent this, so every 50 years there was a systemic correction with debts being canceled, slaves being set free, and every person and family being given back their original allotment of land. The wealth of the land was redistributed and families were reunited for another 50 years.

Jubilee ensured that no one person, family, tribe, or people group would be stuck in the cycle of poverty generation after generation. We often forget that Jubilee also ensured that no one person, family, tribe, or people group would be stuck in the cycle of wealth dependency generation after generation.

Jubilee was radical! Imagine that every 50 years, everyone who has maxed out their credit cards, overextended borrowing for an education, spent all their inheritance, or has difficulty

trying to keep up with a mortgage—everybody's debt is instanta-
neously canceled! Many of us might think, "Those people got into
those situations through their own mistakes. They should get out
on their own!"

In God's Jubilee economy, allowances are made for people's mistakes and bad decisions; it's called grace. People, their children,
and their children's children don't have to live with a legacy of
bad decisions longer than one generation. This is Jubilee and
good news to the poor—because they weren't going to be poor
any longer! The whole concept of Jubilee sounds too good to be
true. And perhaps it is, because unfortunately we have no record
that the people of Israel ever carried it out.

Consider the role of money in our culture, and economic
disparity. In the United States, for example, the official poverty
threshold is $24,000 for a family of four. In 2015, 43 million peo-
ple lived in poverty in the United States, equal to one in seven
Americans living in poverty.[2] Although America's poor are dis-
proportionately people of color who live in urban areas, poverty
numbers are shifting from the cities to the suburbs. Those living
in poverty no longer reside in distant urban centers, but are in the
midst of our churches and communities. They include the most
vulnerable in our society—the elderly, children, and persons with
disabilities.

Can the church be a place of Jubilee, spreading it to our neigh-
bors in our world today? Jubilee is a signal to the world that, un-
like the profit-first model, God's children will be known as people
who are generous, kind, just, restful, and dependent on a loving
and caring God. Jubilee is God's gift to us.

---

2   "Poverty Facts," Poverty USA, accessed February 6, 2017.,
http://www.povertyusa.org/the-state-of-poverty/poverty-facts/.

[Talk about It]

▶ Jubilee is good news to the poor. Discuss how the Scriptures refer to it, and then consider how Jubilee matches up with Western culture's obsession with self.

▶ Are there aspects of Jubilee that could be practiced today? Are there aspects of Jubilee that are not possible to practice today? Consider how Jubilee is outlined in Scripture, and think about your family. What would be the most difficult to embrace? What would be the most life-giving aspect of Jubilee?

▶ Read the following passages and look for similarities, themes, observations, and differences between the authors, contexts, and messages.

Leviticus 25:8-55

Isaiah 61

Luke 4:14-30

2:
[Extending the Vision]

Growing up, I was told not to talk about three things in polite company—politics, religion, and money. Unfortunately, this rule continues to be practiced in society and in the church. Many times the Scripture's call for justice is isolated from our faith walk, politics, and money. This is especially the case when the Scriptures focus on the message of Jubilee.[1]

Jesus read a passage from Isaiah containing the three taboos: politics (allegiance), religion (belonging, beliefs, and behavior), and money (stewardship), for his inaugural address in the polite com-

[**Read Leviticus 25; Isaiah 61; and Luke 4.**]

pany of his home congregation. This wasn't simply an add-on to his ministry or an option for us to take it or leave it. For Jesus, this was a sign of the upside-down kingdom he expressed in the Sermon on the Mount in

---

1   See Leviticus 25; Isaiah 61; and Luke 4.

Matthew 5–7. When he prayed "Your kingdom come. Your will be done, on earth as it is in heaven" (6:10), he envisioned this for us individually, as a church, and in our communities.

> The gospel **(good news)** of Jubilee, which Jesus inaugurated and invites every generation to participate in, is of epic proportions and challenges all our taboos—including money.

My congregation prayerfully discerned that we needed to take a Sabbath year. This meant taking a break from the annual live Christmas nativity program, the Thanksgiving bake and craft sale, the church retreat, weekly Sunday school classes, and midweek prayer meetings. It was hard for us to stop, be still, and connect with God. It was hard to be content and trust God's love for us and who we are as God's good creation. I learned that many of our longtime members, who had served the congregation long before I arrived on scene as the pastor, were tired and in desperate need of Sabbath rest. And I learned that before we can act justly, love mercy, and walk humbly in the ways of God (Micah 6:8), we have to truly know that Jesus is Lord of our time, talents, and our treasures (money).

We dare not divorce Sabbath rest from the Jubilee because one without the other is an incomplete gospel. It is only when we enter into our Sabbath rest that the Jubilee becomes possible.

According to Luke 4:18-19, the Jubilee journey begins when our hearts are in a **vertical** relationship, connected and content with God. It continues as we are in **horizontal** relationships, showing concern and compassion toward others (v. 18). These relational aspects transform both the giver and the receiver (v. 19).

others

> ["The spirit of the Lord God is upon me, because the Lord has anointed me; he has sent me to bring good news to the oppressed, to bind up the brokenhearted, to proclaim liberty to the captives, and release to the prisoners; to proclaim the year of the Lord's favor, and the day of vengeance of our God; to comfort all who mourn" (Isaiah 61:1-2).]

In order to fully appreciate Jesus' inaugural address (Luke 4:18-21), when he preached from Isaiah 61:1-2, we must first understand the perspective of his first-century Jewish audience. Jesus quoted a prophetic passage that promised better days for the Israelites, a broken people who were defeated by the Babylonians and living in exile. The Jews could identify with this passage since they lived under Roman oppression and desperately desired freedom. This Scripture proclaims the beginning of a new time of healing and hope, where the oppressed find freedom and the poor can get back on their feet. This is the year of the Lord's favor—the Jubilee.

[**Read
Luke 4:14-30.**]

God

vertical

horizontal   others

you

Isaiah didn't give up hope. He took up the image of the Jubilee for his generation, speaking of the coming Messiah who would bring about true justice, true healing, true peace, and true Sabbath rest; the Messiah who would bring, once and for all, good news to the poor. Isaiah's Jubilee vision of justice, while still including the fundamental elements of the Levitical Jubilee—justice, sharing, returning home, hospitality, generosity, peace, and Sabbath rest—took on new meaning for the people living in captivity in Babylon.

Luke 4 introduces us to Jesus and his vision for Jubilee. It has evolved into something bigger than both its Levitical origins and Isaiah's messianic prophecy. We see this expanded vision when we read Jesus' Jubilee proclamation, which now included "recovery of sight for the blind." There are a few other things worth noting about the unique way Jesus handled this reading:

> Jesus stopped his reading in the middle of the Isaiah 61:2. This verse goes on to speak about judgement and violent revenge on the enemy. Interestingly, **Jesus left that out**, concluding instead with the Jubilee proclamation of "the year of the Lord's favor," a reference to the Jubilee year as mentioned numerous times in Leviticus.

> In Luke 4:23-27, Jesus recalled stories of the prophets and their interactions with people outside Israel. The widow of Zaraphath and Naaman the Syrian were people who have experienced God's blessings and healing. According to Jesus, the gospel of Jubilee is not just for a closed community of believers. Rather, **it is for everyone**, Gentiles included. This good news wasn't welcomed by Jesus' congregation and almost caused him to lose his life (vv. 28-30).

The original elements in Leviticus and Isaiah's good news of Jubilee remain—rest, justice, sharing, restoration, hospitality, and generosity. Debts are canceled, and slaves are set free. Jesus adds to the long-awaited Jubilee by including:

> physical healing;

> forgiveness of sins; and

> renewal of the individual.

[Talk about It]

▶ Of all the Scripture passages Jesus could have used to inaugurate his ministry (Ten Commandments, the greatest and second commandment, and others), what do you think his reason was for choosing Isaiah 61:1-2? What reasons could Jesus have for ignoring the reference to revenge in the second half of Isaiah 61:2? What is the relationship between revenge and forgiveness when practicing the Jubilee?

▶ The people in Jesus' home synagogue became very angry after the reading and Jesus' explanations. What do you think upset them? In what ways does the gospel of Jubilee still upset the church today?

▶ The gospel of Matthew includes the Sermon on the Mount (chapters 5–7). What upside-down kingdom similarities do you see between Jubilee and the Beatitudes in Matthew 5:1-12? Compare your thoughts with Jesus' teachings in Luke 6:20-26.

▶ Read the Scriptures about the widow of Zarephath (1 Kings 17:8-16) and Naaman the Syrian (2 Kings 5).

> How do these Scriptures relate to Jesus, Jubilee, justice, hospitality, generosity, poverty, and deliverance?

[3: Jesus, Justice, and Jubilee]

As I write this lesson, we are concluding another difficult political season in the United States. It is anticipated that the winning presidential candidate will seek to unite the country through the inaugural address. It will likely include a message of unity while summarizing the administration's agenda and goals and hopes for safety, jobs, and taxes. Ultimately, the message will offer hope and prosperity to those who are able to help themselves.

Jesus' inaugural message in Luke 4 challenges Western political and cultural messages. It shocks our economic sensibilities of safety, security, and wise investment. Instead of sharing the good news to the powerful, privileged, and those already in a position to better themselves, Jesus says the good news of the long-awaited Jubilee is for the poor, imprisoned, blind, and oppressed. The good news of Jubilee is for anyone who recognizes we all are in need of God's help and generosity.

Jesus' ministry of Jubilee addresses the eternal truth of the interconnectedness of justice and salvation, of body and soul, and of faith and works. Jesus calls us to remember the disciplines of Jubilee such as Sabbath, rest, generosity, and healing.

John reports Nathanael's question, "Can anything good come out of Nazareth?" (John 1:46). Jesus noted a version of this question when he said, "No prophet is accepted in the prophet's home-town" (Luke 4:24).

I know how it feels to be deemed unworthy. Some years ago my colleagues and I sat across the desk from a prominent Christian lawyer, from whom we were seeking advice on a business and service venture in our city of Philadelphia. We envisioned a joint urban and suburban program to bring Jubilee for unemployed, underemployed, and formerly incarcerated community people through job creation and training and by providing a sustainable business model. The building would house a thrift store, café, Christian bookstore, art studio, and a church. We believed our area of the city had positive potential. The idea would complement existing thrift stores, and churches would provide a pool of potential workers. Urban populations are traditionally strong thrift store shoppers, and local church leaders would give logistical assistance.

The lawyer's response was chilling. "Let me be frank—there isn't anything good in your city." He went on to say that the people are lazy, the schools are bad and produce criminals, the mayor is a crook, and the streets are all dirty. He advised others to stay away from our city because no one chooses to live there. Outside its art museum, theaters, historical sites, sports stadium, and airport, the lawyer believed our city was no longer relevant to the rest of the region.

The lawyer had volunteered in the city when he was younger, and as a youth he had been optimistic about the future. Since then, however, he had seen a steady decline in the city. He closed with these sobering words: "You have been given jobs and life skills. Where is all that now? What do you have to show for all that?"

> We often separate salvation from justice and money from faith. Yet all of them are included in Jesus' good news.

According to Jesus, Jubilee is a holistic vision encompassing individuals and communities in the promise of *all* things becoming new. The Jubilee kingdom includes good news for:

> the spiritually poor who need God's grace and love, whose lives are empty or falling apart through things they did or things done to them; those dealing with sin, shame, and guilt who need a Savior and new beginning;

> the financially poor who suffer from unjust systems and global violence; and

> those who have accepted Jesus and committed themselves to helping build God's kingdom here on earth—a breaking in of heaven here on earth!

The good news of Jubilee is present in the story of Zacchaeus, whose transformation combined salvation and justice, money and faith (Luke 19). Zacchaeus accepted Jesus' message and agreed to host Jesus at his house. We often forget the next part of the story. Zacchaeus connected his salvation, his newfound faith, to his bank account! Listen to what the good news of Jubilee sounds and looks like: "Zacchaeus stood there and said to the Lord, 'Look, half of my possessions, Lord, I will give to the poor; and if I have defrauded anyone of anything, I will pay back four times as much.' Then Jesus said to him, 'Today salvation has come to this house, because he too is a son of Abraham. For the Son of Man came to seek out and to save the lost'" (Luke 19:8-10).

Zacchaeus's decision to give away half his possessions and repay four times what he had stolen seems excessive, almost crazy. Zacchaeus didn't care if the people were deserving, intelligent, hard workers, or educated. He didn't ask if they would spend the money wisely, invest it, or give it to the church. His response came from his immediate **transformation** and understanding that Jesus' Jubilee message is for everyone, everywhere.

From Zacchaeus's words, we gather that one, he was guilty of taking advantage of the unjust system; two, he felt sorry for his past actions; and three, he was committed to making restitution by bringing about Jubilee. From Jesus' words, we understand that one, Zacchaeus and his household were saved that day and all their sins were forgiven; and two, the key evidence of Zacchaeus's salvation was his public confession and public act of Jubilee.

> Jesus did not separate salvation from justice and Jubilee or separate Zacchaeus's faith from his bank accounts. Perhaps we should do likewise.

[Talk about It]

▶ In your own words, write two or three sentences describing Jesus' good news of Jubilee according to Luke 4 and 19. Share what you wrote with a partner or small group. Discuss the differences and similarities in your descriptions.

▶ Where have you seen salvation (faith) separated from justice? What are the dangers of this separation? How did Jesus speak to this in the Zacchaeus account? What are other examples of this holistic understanding that appear in Scripture?

▶ Write your definition of *salvation*. Where did you learn about this term? Who influenced your understanding of the term?

＞ Do a word study of *salvation* in the Bible. When is it used? Who uses it? Why?

＞ After completing your word study, share what you have learned with someone else. How has your understanding of *salvation* been affected as a result of your study?

4: Moving from Thinking to Doing

Author and theologian

James K. A. Smith challenges the Western notion of discipleship as primarily a "thinking thing," an intellectual pursuit, a belief that simply acquiring more and more knowledge produces our desired change.[1] Even this Bible study, if not lived out in some way, could contribute to the intellectual, didactic approach of discipleship.

---

1   See James K. A. Smith, *You Are What You Love: The Spiritual Power of Habit* (Grand Rapids, MI: Brazos Press, 2016).

Jesus' approach to discipleship and spiritual formation is not merely an intellectual pursuit. Jesus' discipleship and spiritual practices (silence, stillness, solitude, prayer, Sabbath) included the mind (parables, sermons, and penetrating questions). But Jesus also discipled by having his followers participate in **doing**—praying, healing, blessing, feeding people, Sabbath rest, and other ways. Jesus recognized the power of habit, saying "anyone who loves me will obey [do] my teaching" (John 14:23 NIV). Therefore, for the disciples and early church, Jesus, justice, and Jubilee weren't only "thinking things," but also doing, following, and living things.

One Sunday during my first year as pastor, I was standing in front of our church greeting parishioners. I noticed that for every person who entered our building, five or more walked past me

and the church. They were of all ages and races, many carrying bags or pushing carts full of laundry to the laundromat next door. After a few minutes I became painfully aware that even though our congregation had been in the community for over 50 years, this relatively new laundromat was already an asset to this community in ways we didn't know or fully understand.

As I stood to preach, I felt led to put away my prepared sermon notes and share what I had just witnessed. After telling the story I added that if the doors of this laundromat had been closed, people would have been so desperate to get in they would have knocked on its locked doors with the hope that someone would open them. However, if the doors of our church were closed this Sunday, I wasn't as confident that people from our community would even notice, let alone knock on the door, desperate to get in. I closed by inviting the congregation to recognize it was time for us to chart a new direction, to not only be hearers (thinking things) of the Word, but to see it was past time to open our doors (physical and spiritual) and participate in God's Jubilee that was already occurring around us. Eventually a question would emerge, a Jubilee question still guiding our church today, "If God loves the city, and if God loves our congregation—how will they know?"

> "If God loves the city, and if God loves our congregation— how will they know?"

We know from both Scripture and biblical scholars that there is no evidence the Levitical Jubilee ever happened. What we do see in Scripture is the Jubilee (rest, justice, economic sharing, generosity, restoration, hospitality, healing, forgiveness, grace, freedom) that was manifested in Jesus.

But there is more, because the Jubilee did not end with Jesus. In the Gospels we see how the disciples embraced for themselves the inaugural words of Jesus.

> "The Spirit of the Lord is upon me, because he has anointed me to bring good news to the poor. He has sent me to proclaim release to the captives and recovery of sight for the blind, to let the oppressed go free, to proclaim the year of the Lord's favor" (Luke 4:18-19).

These Spirit-filled words would also speak to and guide the disciples in the book of Acts (as they should us today!) to act justly, to love mercy, and to walk humbly with God (Micah 6:8).

It is comforting to see that in the midst of struggles, limited resources, fear, and persecution, the Jubilee was being manifested daily in God's people in very imaginative ways. Alden Bass writes, "The spirit of ancient Israel engulfed the Holy City, and for a brief period of time the utopian community of the Jubilee was reconstituted."[2]

Acts is filled with Jubilee signposts serving as needed reminders that the spirit of Jubilee declared by God through the prophets and echoed by Jesus is now poured out at Pentecost on ordinary people. We have a glimpse of Jesus' vision for Jubilee and justice as it is being passed on from his disciples to the early (Gentile) church, and then to us today. Jubilee was more than a "thinking thing" for the church in Acts. They lived it as well.

---

2   Alden Bass, "The Way," in *Called to Community: The Life Jesus Wants for His People*, ed. Charles E. Moore (Walden, NY: Plough Publishing House, 2016), 55.

Here are signposts of Jubilee recorded in Acts:

> Anointing of the Spirit of the Lord (1–2; 4; 7; 10; 11:19-29; 13–15)

> Good news to the poor—radical generosity and hospitality affecting the financial poor is commonplace (2:42-47; 3:1-10; 4:32-37; 9–10)

> Repentance and restoration to God and one another—ministry of reconciliation (3:11-24; 11; 15; 28)

> Recovery and healing—of the lame, blind, broken, and possessed (3:1-10; 5:12-16; 9:1-19; 19:11-20; 20:7-12)

> Proclaiming freedom for the prisoners (5:12-42; 12:1-18; 16:16-40)

> Setting the oppressed free—transformation of relationships whereby inequities in power and prejudice are addressed and turned upside down (5:1-11; 6:1-7; 8:26–11; 15–16; 18)

> Sabbath rest (13:14, 44; 16:13; 17:2; 18:1-11)

[Talk about It]

▶ For the disciples, Jesus, justice, and Jubilee weren't only thinking things. Instead, they were also to be obeyed and followed; they were to become a habit. How have you personally experienced or seen the gospel limited to being only a thinking thing? What are the problems with this approach?

▶ Discuss how the Spirit led the early church to address the dynamics of power inequity in Acts. Examples can be found in Acts 6:1-7; 8:26–9:43; 11:19-29; 15–16; 18. What can we learn from these examples for our lives and our world today?

▶ Compare the activities in your congregation to those of the church in Acts. What similarities and differences do you see? Is Jubilee a thinking thing or something to obey—a following and doing thing—in your congregation?

▶ Read Acts 4:32-37; 5:1-10.

> Compare and contrast how life comes about through Jubilee (Acts 4:32-37) versus how death comes to Ananias and Sapphira (Acts 5:1-10).

> In what ways do these stories relate to Jubilee and God's justice and generosity?

5:
[Transactions or Transformation?]

My wife and I moved back to Philadelphia after college and joined a local Mennonite church. As a banker, I naturally became church treasurer, overseeing the budget and paying bills. Another important, and surprising, responsibility was keeping track of members who were enrolled in the Brotherly Aid Plan. This was a mutual aid sharing program that acted similarly to car insurance, providing discounts over market insurance rates. To participate in the plan, one needed to regularly attend church. I followed up with those who weren't regular attenders to let them know they were jeopardizing their eligibility for this plan.

After the Brotherly Aid Plan became insolvent, it came as no surprise that attendance dropped in many congregations. Years later, it's easy to see how the plan, congregations, members, and church treasurers fell into the trap of seeing each other as transactions.

Good intentions aside, when faith relationships are primarily transactional, people see themselves as transactions, as sources of production and revenue. Jesus' Jubilee is different because it presents transformation as people over production, and relationships over revenue. A Jubilee framework seeks to implement a mutual aid concept where some will, and should, give more so those who have less can benefit. But the ultimate hope and expectation is that those who are helped today will be equipped to give more as they experience restoration.

Our congregation has a six-week summer program, which runs all day, Monday to Friday. We provide experiences such as art, drama, choir, library club, trips, games, and lunch for several dozen children ages 8 to 13. The staff includes adult volunteers

from our congregation, a paid summer worker, a college student paid with grant money, and me. Our nonprofit organization provides funds for supplies, trips, and other items.

Near the end of the third summer of the program, a community liaison wanted to meet with me. I was warmly greeted at her house by four women from the community. They fed me and thanked me and our church and nonprofit organization for our commitment to the community. Then they said something I needed to hear, "Pastor Leonard, you have to stop giving all this summer stuff to us for free, because we need, and want, to help."

I was speechless—a first for me. As a pastor I railed against both secular and sacred oppressive systems that kept communities of color dependent instead of empowered and set free. Yet I was repeating the same oppressive behavior, failing to see the unique, God-given assets and gifts in the people in our community. After asking the women to accept my apology, I listened to their insights into the ways we could collaborate in a more holistic and Jubilee manner. Their suggestions included an orientation outlining expectations and opportunities to help, charging a nominal fee for trips and having those who could not afford to pay volunteer as chaperones, and asking parents and guardians to help set up or clean up lunch. I feverishly jotted down their ideas. Later that day I journaled about truly experiencing Jubilee as I received good news, forgiveness, hospitality, and restoration.

> As a pastor I railed against both secular and sacred oppressive systems that kept communities of color dependent instead of empowered and set free. Yet I was repeating the same oppressive behavior.

Jubilee represents our God's desire for each of us to experience healthy relationships (with God, with others, with ourselves, and with creation) here on earth (Leviticus 25; Isaiah 61:1-4; Luke 4:18-19). Our focus is frequently on our relationship with God, but we need to examine other relationships as well. We are to look at the conditions of our souls, our relationships with others (friend and foe), and our relationships with God's good creation.

> We can no longer settle for unjust relationships where we individually, or as a community, maintain our position of power and control, where we are always in the position of giving. Likewise, we cannot settle any longer for unjust relationships where individuals or communities are systematically kept in the position of always receiving help.

The good news of Jubilee is that in all our relationships we are invited to first submit to God, and then to one another in love. When we do this we can no longer settle for unjust relationships where we individually, or as a community, maintain our position of power and control, where we are always in the position of giving. Likewise, we cannot settle any longer for unjust relationships where individuals or communities are systematically kept in the position of always receiving help. Jubilee, like Pentecost, truly occurs when our relationships and systems are turned **upside down** and **inside out!** Jubilee demands we go beyond superficial and only transactional relationships, in which we often keeping people at arm's length, in our piety and charity. Rather, Jubilee invites us to the discomfort of moving ourselves and our communities towards intimate, transformational relationships—relationships where we can begin to see ourselves as God sees us, where we can begin to see others as God sees them, and where we begin to see more clearly how God is actively seeking to engage our world through us.

One sign a relationship is transactional, rather than transformational, is if the power dynamics remain the same over an extended period of time. This is not Jubilee. This type of relationship makes the giver (church, mission agency, individual) feel good and might even help the receiver at some immediate, tangible level. But Jubilee requires **we extend the same grace** given to us willingly by God, and that we creatively position ourselves as both receivers and givers, both helpers and the helped, both forgivers and the forgiven (Acts 6:1-7).

We see this in the Gospels when Jesus willingly and creatively positioned himself to receive from the same people who received from him. One of these places was in Bethany at the home of Mary, Martha, and Lazarus. Jesus knew they would take care of him. If Jesus, who would give his life on the cross for us, recognized his need to experience the gift of receiving hospitality and the blessing of being anointed by women (Luke 7:36-50; Matthew 26:6-13), shouldn't we willingly and creatively position ourselves to be receivers as well?

[Talk about It]

▶ Which relationships are easier to involve ourselves in—transactional or transformational? Which of the two would best describe your ministry and community relationships?

▶ Read about Peter, John, and the beggar in Acts 3. What are the benefits of this transformational relationship? What are the costs of this transformational relationship? Allow this story to guide you in thinking about charity, dependency, empowerment, and boundaries.

▶ Make two columns on a piece of paper, one labeled "Transaction" and the other labeled "Transformation."

> Read Leviticus 25; Isaiah 61:1-4; Luke 4:18-19.

> Which of the aspects of the Jubilee described in these passages are transactional (production and revenue) and which are transformational (people and relational)? Write them in the appropriate columns.

Transaction	Transformation

> From this exercise, what does Scripture teach about Jubilee?

6:
[Creating Space for Jubilee]

My family and I spent one of my sabbaticals in Puerto Rico, where my wife, Rosalie, was born and grew up. While Rosalie did research at the university and my daughters attended school, my toddler son and I visited the plazas, the centerpieces of Puerto Rico's small towns and cities. **Las plazas** offer a haven from the heat of the day and a place to rest among beautiful tropical plants, such as large mango and avocado trees and other vegetation. Children, teens, families, and the elderly visit the plazas while musicians perform, artists show their work, students study, elderly women knit, and older men play dominoes. Small businesses surround the plaza, including social services, stores, and schools for children and adults. At the northern end of every plaza is a Catholic church that built, funds, and manages the plaza. The church's doors are always open for rest, worship, silence, prayer, a hot meal, clothing, or sanctuary.

Las plazas remind me of Jesus' holistic Jubilee vision where individuals and communities receive the promise that all things are becoming new. The plaza model inspired our church in Philadelphia, and so we created space for stillness, Sabbath, prayer, salvation, healing, rest, restoration, feeding people, and economic sharing and development. Daily, we bear witness that this is the year of Jubilee!

One gift of urban living is the cultural and ethnic diversity. Our congregation's community, Oxford Circle, was recently designated the most diverse area in Philadelphia. Yet diversity presents real challenges, such as understanding one another and appreciating cultural differences, languages, and practices. All cultures seem to have two things in common, however—a love of food and fellowship.

We talked with parents of children in our after-school programs, adults in our high school equivalency classes and English language classes, and members of the local business community about hosting an outdoor Spring Food Fair on our property to celebrate the community's diversity. Now an annual event that also includes a 5K run, the food fair allows us to celebrate diversity, inspire a sense of shared belonging, and eat good food from

> By creating the space for this event, we, the givers, receive; the powerless gain power; and Jesus, justice, and Jubilee are manifested.

Germany, Haiti, Cameroon, Puerto Rico, Brazil, Korea, Syria, and Palestine, just to name a few places. Equally important, the food fair is a fundraiser for the programs that our nonprofit organization sponsors.

By creating the space for this event, we, the givers, receive; the powerless gain power; and Jesus, justice, and Jubilee are manifested. The same individuals and businesses we are blessed to minister to are empowered on this day to minister to us by raising funds that will ultimately directly benefit them and the larger community.

John M. Perkins embodies Jubilee, encouraging congregations to become beloved communities of God. He cites **three Rs of community development**.[1] They encapsulate the Jubilee gospel framework and begin with us, the church, embracing the gospel of Jubilee and living it out in our congregations and communities.

1. Relocation: God relocated from heaven to earth in the form of Jesus, and then traveled from one area to the next to bring about Jubilee and plant the seeds of community. For some, relocation might mean physically moving from our current residence to another area to more faithfully live out the Jubilee. For others, relocation does not require a physical move, but a relocation of

---

1   From John M. Perkins, "What Is Christian Community Development?," in *Restoring At-Risk Communities: Doing It Together and Doing It Right*, ed. John M. Perkins (Grand Rapids, MI: Baker Books, 1995), 21–23.

focus from the inside of the church to the outside. Perkins believes "living the gospel means desiring for your neighbor and your neighbor's family that which you desire for yourself and your family. . . . Living the gospel means sharing in the the suffering and pain of others. . . . Relocation transforms 'you, them, and theirs' to 'we, us, and ours.' "[2]

> "Living the gospel means sharing in the suffering and pain of others. . . . Relocation transforms 'you, them, and theirs' to 'we, us, and ours.'"

2. Reconciliation: This begins with people being reconciled to God through Christ. Only then can Spirit-led reconciliation occur neighbor to neighbor, people to people, and church to community. The Jubilee gospel of Jesus requires dismantling barriers so Christians can work toward shalom and a truly shared and just community. Author and theologian Drew Hart reminds us that "The church must be a place where we take seriously the call to nonconformity in the way of Jesus. In doing so, we are drawn into further solidarity with the poor, oppressed, and 'lowly.' "[3]

> "The church must be a place where we take seriously the call to nonconformity in the way of Jesus. In doing so, we are drawn into further solidarity with the poor, oppressed, and 'lowly.'"

2   Ibid., 21–22.
3   Drew Hart, *Trouble I've Seen: Changing the Way the Church Views Racism* (Harrisonburg, VA: Herald Press, 2016), 141.

3. Redistribution: Jubilee requires a strategic and creative redistribution of resources through partnership and economic development. This commitment does not come from a government-mandated endeavor where things are forcefully taken from one person and given to another. Rather, it requires people of faith to willingly use their skills, education, and resources and to put them to work empowering all people in the church and larger community. This includes redistribution of our time and talents to local schools and community nonprofits. It includes redistribution of our networks and education by providing access to mentors and internships to those on the margins. And it includes redistribution of power so that people and communities can be totally set free from the grip of poverty and injustice.

> This commitment . . . requires people of faith to willingly use their skills, education, and resources and to put them to work empowering all people in the church and larger community.

I believe church-sponsored *las plazas* can help our congregations live out the three Rs and, more importantly, the Jubilee. We can create spaces for gathering, healing, sanctuary, worship, and commerce. We can become safe spaces for artists, families, children, the elderly, the poor, the broken, and those recently released from prison. We can relocate our homes, time, money, and hearts so we become Jubilee models of reconciliation and redistribution.

[Talk about It]

▶ In what ways does the plaza model of generosity resonate with you and your understanding of being the church together? Forget practical aspects, and spend several minutes dreaming about what this plaza would look like in your context. How would Jubilee be shown in this endeavor?

▶ What aspects of the three Rs do you resonate with? Which aspects present challenges?

▶ What are you going to do with what you learned about Jubilee?

> Make a list of things you learned, either on paper or in your mind. Then, challenge yourself to find one concrete way to put at least one of your learnings into practice.

> Find one person to share with about what you will practice. Ask that person to pray for you and encourage you as you put your learning into practice.

[About the Writer]

Leonard Dow has been the pastor at Oxford Circle Mennonite
Church (OCMC) in Northeast Philadelphia for almost 20 years.
A graduate of Eastern Mennonite University, he worked in retail
banking before becoming a pastor.

During Leonard's time at OCMC, the congregation has been
blessed by God to continue to grow in its vision of embracing and
seeing the Jubilee, as portrayed in Luke 4. This happens in direct
ways through its nonprofit Oxford Circle Christian Community
Development Association, which offers programs and services
designed to address the needs of the community. Jubilee also
affects the congregation through the gift of growth in the diversity of ethnicities, educational levels, and religious backgrounds
of those who worship together.

Leonard is board chair of Oxford Circle Christian Community
Development Association, vice chair of Mennonite Central
Committee U.S. board, chair of Kingdom Builder's Network of
Greater Philadelphia, and bishop of the Philadelphia District of
Lancaster Mennonite Conference.

Most importantly, however, Leonard loves the Lord. He is
married to Dr. Rosalie Rolon-Dow and they have three children,
Carmela, Marcela, and Lorenzo.

CPSIA information can be obtained
at www.ICGtesting.com
Printed in the USA
BVOW09s1119110517

483657BV00001BA/32/P

9 781513 801575

UPSIDE DOWN LIVING

money

Weary of Christian faith wrapped in a flag and trapped in your heart?
Tired of faith as usual?

Live out your Christian faith through the lens of Jesus. Follow values that seem so countercultural they appear to be upside down. Each compelling six-session Upside-Down Living Bible study helps us encounter the teachings of Jesus and wrestle with living out the kingdom here and now. The Bible isn't a cookbook with solutions for every ethical dilemma, but it helps us raise the right questions, encounter the teachings of Jesus, and discover new ways of faithful living in the world. Ideal for Sunday school or Bible study sessions, each topical study covers a specific theme or issue and comes with thought-provoking discussion questions and activities. Be inspired and transformed in your faith. Live upside down.

Every day we face decisions that affect our wallets—and these decisions say a lot about our priorities. The way we use money can communicate power and strength, charity and selflessness. How do your decisions about the use of money and resources reflect or expand your faith? This study takes an honest look at financial choices and economics through the lens of Jubilee, highlighting how the community and the world around you can be affected by your decisions.

ISBN 978-1-5138-0157-5

Herald Press
www.heraldpress.com

50999

9 781513 801575

$9.99 USD